SPEAK UNTIL
JUSTICE WAKES

PROPHETIC REFLECTIONS FROM
J. ALFRED SMITH SR.

J. ALFRED SMITH SR.

EDITED BY JINI M. KILGORE

JUDSON PRESS
PUBLISHERS SINCE 1824

VALLEY FORGE

SPEAK UNTIL JUSTICE WAKES:
Prophetic Reflections from J. Alfred Smith Sr.

© 2006 by Judson Press, Valley Forge, PA 19482-0851
All rights reserved.

The author and Judson Press have made every effort to trace the ownership of all quotes. In the event of a question arising from the use of a quote, we regret any error made and will be pleased to make the necessary correction in future printings and editions of this book.

Library of Congress Cataloging-in-Publication Data
Smith, J. Alfred (James Alfred)
  Speak until justice wakes : prophetic reflections / from J. Alfred Smith, Sr. ; edited by Jini Kilgore.
      p. cm.
ISBN 0-8170-1501-9 (pbk. : alk. paper) 1. Sermons, American--African American authors. 2. Baptists--Sermons. I. Kilgore, Jini. II. Title.
BX6452.S66 2006
252'.061--dc22   2006017854

Printed in the U.S.A.

14 13 12 11 10 09 08 07 06   10 9 8 7 6 5 4 3 2 1

DEDICATION

THIS BOOK IS AFFECTIONATELY DEDICATED TO THE MEMORY OF Amy Elnora Smith, my mother, and to Willie Joe and Olivia Goodwin, the father and mother of Joanna, my wife, three people who upheld us with their prayers and shared wisdom; and to the memory of Dr. Thomas Kilgore and Dr. William Augustus Jones, whose wisdom gave us the courage to be true to the highest and the best when we were at our wit's end; and to the many students who have listened and shared precious classroom time with us.

DR. J. ALFRED SMITH SR.
Senior Pastor, Allen Temple Baptist Church
Oakland, California
Distinguished Senior Professor
of Preaching and Church Ministries
American Baptist Seminary of the West and
The Graduate Theological Union
Berkeley, California

CONTENTS

FOREWORD

OVER THE COURSE OF NEARLY SIXTY YEARS OF MINISTERIAL CALL-
ing, Pastor J. Alfred Smith Sr. has consistently preached and
lived an ethic that is true to prophetic ministry. Some years
ago, in the infancy of my own ministry, I remember an experience with him in the East Oakland, California, parish where
God had planted him to serve as pastor. One day as we slowly rode together down the despair-ridden streets, surveying
the desolation and pain in the faces of the people, I asked him,
"Dad, why is it that some of our leaders and preachers fail to
speak about injustice in the land?"

He simply responded, "Son, to do so requires moral commitment."

I am a witness that throughout his ministry, J. Alfred Smith
Sr. has demonstrated an unwavering sense of moral commitment that compels him to speak prophetic truth to power
through his sermonic tears and lamentations and through his
thunderous, fiery calls to community action.

The essays in this book represent a wide range of prophetic outpouring and inspiration from the heart and soul of J.
Alfred Smith Sr. They reflect his great courage in taking ethical stands that were often unpopular initially, and that were
sometimes met with threats of reprisal. The writings are
clearly steeped in prayer and spirituality as Dr. Smith, like his

cherished teacher Dr. Howard Thurman, shines a light on the inextricable connection between the realms of spirituality and social justice. Thus, the challenging thoughts expressed here appeal to the hearts of faithful people, calling us amid the noisy clatter of the world to hear "the voice of one crying out in the wilderness, 'Prepare the way of the Lord'" (Matthew 3:3).

One of the common problems with prophetic messages and messengers is that they sometimes overwhelm their audiences with the magnitude of injustice in the world, leaving us as individuals with the feeling that there is nothing we can do to make a difference. Dr. Smith's messages, however, help us to actively embrace the popular motto "Think globally and act locally." They return us to the very attainable prophetic requirement placed on us by Scripture that we "do justice, and . . . love kindness, and . . . walk humbly with [our] God" (Micah 6:8). Finally, these essays challenge and empower us to arise from apathy and to remove the self-imposed shackles of futility, for as Dr. Smith often exclaims, "It is time to get up from the rocking chair of lazy religion!"

J. ALFRED SMITH JR., D.MIN.
Senior Pastor, Antioch Baptist Church
San Jose, California
Lecturer, Africana Religion
San Francisco State University

ACKNOWLEDGMENTS

I am deeply indebted to the Reverend Jini Kilgore, who served as my editor. Not enough can be said about the high professionalism and the guidance and patience of Randy Frame and Rebecca Irwin-Diehl of Judson Press, whose expertise made this manuscript possible.

DR. J. ALFRED SMITH SR.
Senior Pastor, Allen Temple Baptist Church
Oakland, California
Distinguish Senior Professor of
Preaching and Church Ministries
American Baptist Seminary of the West
and the Graduate Theological Union
Berkeley, California

[1]
A CALL TO ACTION
IN AN UNSAFE WORLD

Based on Lamentations 1:1-2

How lonely sits the city
that once was full of people!
How like a widow she has become,
she that was great among the nations!
She that was a princess among the provinces
has become a vassal.
Lamentations 1:1

ONE COULD EASILY CONTEND THAT THERE IS NO SAFE PLACE TO be in this world. As the terrorists' destruction of the Twin Towers proved, the workplace is not safe. The world of pension security is fragile, as employees of Enron will testify. The world of pharmacology is dangerous, as demonstrated by overpriced drugs, some with deadly side effects. The world of water carries life-threatening bacteria; the world of soil is laden with harmful pesticides that lodge in the food that comes from the earth. The world of business is risky, given that some extortion-minded patrons will go so far as to sue a restaurant for serving too-hot coffee.

Lamentations suggests that the world of the city is not safe:

Oh, oh, oh . . .
How empty the city, once teeming with people.
A widow, this city, once in the front rank of nations,
once queen of the ball, she's now a drudge in the kitchen.

She cries herself to sleep each night, tears soaking her pillow.
No one's left among her lovers to sit and hold her hand.
Her friends have all dumped her.
Lamentations 1:1-2 MESSAGE

When I read this passage, I cannot help but think of one of our nation's most venerable cities—New Orleans. And in thinking of New Orleans, I am reminded that of all the unsafe places to be in this world, perhaps the most unsafe place is to be poor, especially for those who happen to be persons of color. The plight of the poor was highlighted in 2005 by our country's most devastating natural disaster, Hurricane Katrina.

Lessons from Katrina will remain with us for a long time. After the hurricane, Congress and the White House indicated that they would not initiate new measures to aid the poor. Instead, they said they would push to reduce the costs of existing programs that help the poor, programs such as Medicaid and food stamps—this at a time when thousands of evacuees from Louisiana, Mississippi, and Alabama needed these programs more than ever. But cuts were deemed necessary to finance an ongoing war in Iraq.

In addition to the devastating budget cuts made in service programs, federal guidelines allowed contractors in the hurricane-ravaged areas to hire construction workers who work for less than the going rate. No policy guidelines were put in place to protect the rights of the local workers, nor was any guarantee given that local minority contractors would be given a fair share of the subcontracts.

The post-Katrina images of hurting people have faded from our minds. The news media no longer focus their cameras on those who lost their loved ones, their jobs, and in some cases all they possessed. But the truth is that long after the poor— black Americans in particular but also poor people of other ethnic groups, including forgotten white people—have become invisible again, the physical, emotional, economic, and spiritual wounds that this tragedy hurled on the underclass will remain. What's more, the Halliburton-type companies of the world will continue to do business, making lots of money, even as the number of people without health insurance continues to increase by hundreds of thousands per year.

Local churches can do only so much. It is time for a prophetic word to the nation. It is time for courageous people to stand up and be counted, to call for a change in our country's priorities. In short, *people* priorities must take precedence over the priorities of national and multinational corporations.

Those who preach in the name of the lowly Nazarene must remember that Jesus was not a prosperity gospel preacher. In his inaugural sermon, his message was,

"The Spirit of the LORD is upon Me,
Because he has anointed Me to preach the gospel to the poor;
He has sent Me to heal the brokenhearted,
To proclaim liberty to the captives
And recovery of sight to the blind,
To set at liberty those who are oppressed;
To proclaim the acceptable year of the LORD."
Luke 4:18-21 NKJV

Many of the "sheroes" and heroes of ages past modeled for us the kind of ministry that speaks truth to power. Among them are Sojourner Truth, Harriet Tubman, Jarena Lee, Ida B. Wells Barnett, Mary McLeod Bethune, Frederick Douglass, Walter White, Medgar Evers, Fannie Lou Hamer, and Martin Luther King Jr.

We must make it a priority to recruit and mentor young women and men to take up the calling others have modeled, a calling to serve all people evenly and equally. In so doing, we must remember that Jesus never endorsed Caesar, nor did Jesus trust Caesar to elevate his people to higher plateaus of living.

When we come to the end of our earthly days, may we look back at the way we lived and conclude that we lived with courage, so that we might say with the apostle Paul, "We have fought the good fight. We have finished the race. We have kept the faith."

[2]
DELIVER US FROM EVIL

Based on Matthew 6:13

"Lead us not into temptation, but deliver us from evil."
Matthew 6:13 KJV
"Do not bring us to hard testing, but keep us safe from
the Evil One."
Matthew 6:13 GNT

MAYA ANGELOU, REMINDING US THAT EVIL IS THE STRONGEST
enemy facing urban America, writes, "In these bloody and
frightful nights when an urban warrior can find no face more
despicable than his own, no ammunition more deadly than
self-hate, and no target more deserving of his true aim than
his brother, we must wonder how we came so late and only
to this place."[1]

It was evil that brought us to the ugly place of self-destruction. It is evil that makes us work hard at destroying each
other. It is evil that seeks to defame our past, dismantle our
present, and deny our future. Evil is God's ancient foe,
nature's ecological assassin, and humanity's cold-blooded
exterminator.

I am well acquainted with evil, having grown up during the cross-burning days of the Ku Klux Klan, skinheads, the White Citizens' Council, and other racist groups. But I never thought I'd live to fear young black males who look like me yet bring a kind of black terrorism to the inner-city neighborhood of the church I serve as pastor. Due to black terrorism, Allen Temple has to have more meetings during the day because elderly women and single parents are afraid to cross International Boulevard in East Oakland to attend a meeting at night.

No sophisticated scholar, no untutored failure, no well-to-do stockbroker, no bankrupt creditor, no serious saint, no stained sinner, no inexperienced young person, and no seasoned veteran can escape the captivity of evil. The wisest wisdom, the fastest feet, and the strongest strength are no match for evil. This is why Jesus told us to pray for deliverance from evil: "Keep us safe from the Evil One" (Matthew 6:13 GNT).

Because evil is the one shoe that fits every foot, Jesus teaches that each of us is to pray, "Deliver us from evil." No one has a franchise to pray, "Deliver *me* from evil." No one has a permit of spiritual superiority to pray, "Deliver *them* from evil." And no person has been authorized to pray, "Deliver *her* or *him* from evil." Since everyone is a prisoner of war in the stockade of Satan, God's power of deliverance is needed.

Deliver us, great God. We are no match for masterful evil. Too many of us are in the captivity of evil. Our mouths declare evil. Our manners depict evil. Our morals display evil.

Deliver us, God Almighty. Too many of us are dying from addictive dependency to evil. Like a poisonous snake, evil is biting us with the devotion of a deadly killer. Like a cancer, evil is quietly eating our spiritual cells.

Deliver us, God our Redeemer. Evil blinds our moral sight and our spiritual insight. Evil deafens our ears to the plain truth of the preached word. Evil paralyzes the legs of those who would walk in the pathways of righteousness.

Keep us safe, merciful God, from the Evil One who would destroy the taste buds that hunger and thirst after righteousness. Protect us, prayer-hearing God, from the Evil One who desires the destruction of our prayer-regulated nervous system so that we would become spiritual paraplegics. Deliver us as only you can do. Deliver us from evil. Deliver us from defeat to determination, from fear to faith, from greed to generosity, from grumbling to grace. Deliver us from evil.

How does God deliver us from evil? First, God delivers us from the evil that hides in our hearts. God works with those who ask him by giving us a clean heart. Just as those whose bodies are clean must bathe daily with soap and water, Christians must use the soap of confession for the cleansing of our hearts.

Recall the lesson in 1 John 1:8-9: "If we say we have no sin, we are only fooling ourselves and refusing to accept the truth. But if we confess our sins to him, he is faithful and just to forgive us and to cleanse us from every wrong" (NLT).

Pride often prevents us from cleansing. Pride is self-devotion and self-justification. Pride points us to everybody's sin but our own. Pride is the sin of self-deception. Pride separates us from God.

When we are separated from God, we reject God as the Lord of our lives. When we reject God as the Lord of our lives, we are free to deny God as the Lord of our brothers and sisters. Having rejected God as the Lord of our brothers and sisters, we then make ourselves the lord of our brothers and sisters, judging them with envy and jealousy, managing them with criticism, undercutting them with betrayal, and destroying them with malice. Only God can deliver us from the evil of hearts filled with pride and self-righteousness.

Second, God will deliver us from the evil that comes to us from our enemies. Psalm 38:12-16 (NLT) explains how our enemies work to destroy our spirit and defame our reputation:

"Meanwhile, my enemies lay traps for me;
they make plans to ruin me.
They think up treacherous deeds all day long.
But I am deaf to all their threats.
I am silent before them as one who cannot speak.
I choose to hear nothing,
and I make no reply.

For I am waiting for you, O LORD.
You must answer for me, O Lord my God.
I prayed, "Don't let my enemies gloat over me
or rejoice at my downfall."

The psalmist reminds us that we do not know how to fight our enemies. Our task is to love and not hate, to forgive and not seek revenge, to return evil with goodness, and to trust God to fight all of our battles.

J. B. Phillips translates Romans 12:19-21 this way: "Never take vengeance into your own hands, my dear friends: stand back and let God punish if he will. For it is written: 'Vengeance is mine. I will repay.' And these are God's words: 'Therefore, if your enemy hungers, feed him; if he thirsts, give him a drink; for in so doing you will heap coals of fire on his head.' Don't allow yourself to be overpowered with evil. Take the offensive—overpower evil by good!"

You might respond by asking, "What about my secret enemies? There are people who smile in my face but harm me behind my back." My response is that you don't know who your secret enemies are, and I don't know who mine are. But we can obey Jesus and pray, "Deliver us from evil." Don't talk to other people about your enemies. Talk to God about them. You can pray Psalm 35, which begins, "O Lord, fight those fighting me; declare war on them for their attacks on me. Put on your armor, take your shield and protect me by standing in front" (TLB).

When we ask him, God delivers us from the evil that hides in our hearts. God is our janitor who takes out the trash that is in our hearts. God washes our minds of evil thoughts. God cleanses our tongues to speak with kindness. God makes us righteous in our dealings with one another. God delivers us from false friends, from ugly and mean enemies, and from those who would seek to harm us. God delivers us and keeps us from being corrupted by an evil world. Jesus prayed that you and I would not be corrupted by this evil world: "Now I am leaving the world, and leaving them behind, and coming to you. Holy Father, keep them in your care—all those you have given me—so that they will be united just as we are, with none missing. During my time here I have kept safe within your family all of these you gave me. I guarded them so that not one perished, except the son of hell, as the Scriptures foretold" (John 17:11-12 TLB).

Jesus prayed for you and me. He prayed that you and I would not be corrupted by this corrupt world. Everywhere there is corruption in the land. Corruption stalks the streets like a gang leader. Evil enters our lives at every turn. We meet evil at school, at work, at home, and in the church. We find it in our movies, in our newspapers, in our music, and in our television programs. But remember that Jesus prayed for you and for me. God, if we are willing, will deliver us from being corrupted by an evil world.

Take courage. Pray that God will "deliver us from evil." The prayer is short enough to remember. The words are simple enough for us to pronounce. Ask God to deliver us from evil ground, for God wants us to mix and mingle with people who live on higher ground. Our environment can harm or help us. Our associations can contaminate or challenge us. Our peer group can destroy or develop us. Psalm 1 says, "Blessed is the man that walketh not in the counsel of the ungodly, nor standeth in the way of sinners, nor sitteth in the seat of the scornful" (KJV).

Hear the words of the hymn writer Johnson Oatman Jr.:

I'm pressing on the upward way,
New heights I'm gaining every day.

Still praying as I'm onward bound,
"Lord, plant my feet on higher ground."

My heart has no desire to stay
Where doubts arise and fears dismay;
Though some may dwell where those abound,
My prayer, my aim, is higher ground.

I want to live above the world,
Though Satan's darts at me are hurled;
For faith has caught the joyful sound,
The song of saints on higher ground.

I want to scale the utmost height,
And catch a gleam of glory bright;
But still I'll pray till heaven I've found,
"Lord, plant my feet on higher ground."

Refrain
Lord, lift me up and let me stand,
By faith, on heaven's tableland
A higher plane than I have found;
Lord, plant my feet on higher ground.[2]

NOTES
1. Maya Angelou. "I Dare to Hope," in *Even the Stars Look Lonesome* (New York: Barnes & Noble, 1998), 101.
2. Johnson Oatman Jr., "Higher Ground," 1898, public domain.

[3]
THE SCARS OF MINISTRY

Based on Luke 24:33-42

From now on, let no one make trouble for me; for I carry the marks of Jesus branded on my body.
Galatians 6:17

MINISTERING IN THE NAME OF JESUS IS A JOYFUL OPPORTUNITY, but for those who seek to tell the truth, it can also be an occasion for suffering. To put it bluntly, Christian ministry will result in scars, even when those who are ministering in the name of Jesus are doing their best and are doing it "right."

To understand this point, we need look no further than Jesus' ministry. The scars he received were not a result of any imperfection in his character or a lack of quality in his ministry. There was no blight in the Lord's bones, no chicanery in his conduct, no culpability in his character, no default in his deeds, no defilement in his doings, no doubt in his devotion, no evil in his eye, no hatred in his heart. Still, the forces of evil pierced the holy hands that had healed and helped. They pierced the beautiful feet that had preached the gospel of peace.

Likewise, all who follow Jesus, including those who pastor God's people, will have scars on their souls to show that, like Jesus who called them, they have been wounded by many of the same people they have tried to assist, to bless, to coach, to direct, to encourage, to fertilize with the faith, to guide, to help, to inform, and to inspire. Scars are visible symbols that some people are out to demoralize, defame, defeat, and destroy those who seek to utter a prophetic word.

Remember, however, that scars are also visible signs that those who sought to destroy did not succeed in their efforts. For a scar is evidence of a wound that has healed.

Ultimately, a scar is a sign of your love for Jesus and your willingness to serve. You serve in love because Jesus was wounded for your sins and for mine; he was wounded *by* your sins and mine. There is an old legend about Satan appearing to a saint and declaring, "I am the Christ." Wisely, the saint responds by asking, "Where are the marks of the nails?"

Let me conclude with these words, attributed to United Methodist Bishop Brenton Thoburn Badley:

Lord, when I am weary with toiling,
And burdensome seem Thy commands,
If my load should lead to complaining,
Lord, show me Thy hands—
Thy nail-pierced hands, Thy cross-torn hands,
My Saviour, show me Thy hands.

Christ, if ever my footsteps should falter,
And I be prepared for retreat,
If desert or thorn cause lamenting,
Lord, show me Thy feet—
Thy bleeding feet, Thy nail-scarred feet,
My Jesus, show me Thy feet.

Oh, God, dare I show Thee
My hands and my feet?[1]

NOTE
1. Brenton Thoburn Badley, "Show Me Thy Hands,"
http://www.joyful ministry.com/handst.htm (accessed April 6, 2006).

[4]
SPEAK UNTIL JUSTICE WAKES

Based on Jeremiah 38:1-13

Ebed-melech the Ethiopian, a eunuch in the king's house, heard that they had put Jeremiah into the cistern. The king happened to be sitting at the Benjamin Gate, So Ebed-melech left the king's house and spoke to the king.
Jeremiah 38:7-8

PROPHETIC PREACHING, IN ESSENCE, IS PREACHING THAT SPEAKS truth to power. Prophetic preaching provides steel for the spines of the powerless. Prophetic preaching is a thermostat, not a thermometer. It not only calls for integrity in private ethical and moral behavior, but it calls for ethical consistency in public policy and practice.

As early as 1823, Daniel Webster called for the prophetic in American social practice:

> If truth be not diffused error will be; if God and His Word are not known and received, the devil and his works will gain the ascendancy; if the evangelical volume does not reach every hamlet, the pages of a corrupt and

licentious literature will; if the power of the Gospel is not felt throughout the length and breadth of the land, anarchy and misrule, degradation and misery, corruption and darkness will reign without mitigation or end.[1]

Because of a paucity of prophetic preaching, Webster's fearful vision has become an unwelcome reality, not only in the high places of corporate America and Wall Street, where financial giants are being exposed, but also in other areas of public institutional life. Nevertheless, the flickering flames of prophetic preaching in the black tradition are being fueled by Iva V. Carruthers, Jeremiah Wright Jr., Freddie Haynes, and many others. Among their venues is the annual Samuel DeWitt Proctor Conference on Church Development and Prophetic Ministry. Since the death of Dr. Martin Luther King Jr., black theologians and womanist scholars have served as prophetic voices in the academy even as some pastors of black megachurches who seek acceptance in high political circles have elected to privatize their religious beliefs and practices so as to avoid confrontation with national public policymakers.

In light of these trends, Jeremiah 38:1-13 has special relevance for the black church today. During the reign of King Zedekiah of Judah, the nation experienced a crisis. Nebuchadnezzar, king of Babylon, was about to attack Jerusalem, the religious center of Judah. Judah turned for help to its ally Egypt, but Egypt couldn't help because it had troubles at home. King Zedekiah turned to the prophets for a word, but two prophetic schools of theology were at odds with each other and gave conflicting advice to the king.

The school of thought led by the false prophet Hananiah predicted a positive picture of Judah's victory over Babylon. But the school of thought led by the prophet Jeremiah predicted national defeat. Appearing to be antipatriotic and pro-Babylonian, Jeremiah was hauled off to prison, where he was considered to be dangerous and was placed in "the hole," a dungeon where there was plenty of mud but no water. Our text informs us that Jeremiah sank into the mud and became motionless, even lacking food and water to sustain himself.

But God raised up a "layperson" with a prophetic ministry to help Jeremiah. This servant was a low-ranking resident of the king's house. One might say he was *in* the king's house but not *of* it. His ethical and moral values transcended the politics of the house. His name was Ebed-melech. In Hebrew, *Ebed* means "servant," and *melech* means "king." This Ethiopian—this black man—was considered less than a man by many, not only because his skin was black, but also because he had been castrated and thus was unable to father children. He did not, however, define himself by his sexual inability. Rather, he showed himself to be a man by virtue of his courage to speak to King Zedekiah as the servant of the King of kings: "My lord the king, these men have done evil in all that they have done to Jeremiah the prophet, whom they have cast into the dungeon; and he is like to die for hunger in the place where he is: for there is no more bread in the city" (Jeremiah 38:9 KJV).

This low-level Ethiopian eunuch stood up to four men of the king's cabinet, speaking truth to power. Because he was in the house but not of the house, speaking truth to power was a priority for him. The position he held did not matter. Ebedmelech's respect for God's prophet was most admirable. By doing what he was called to do, he became a role model who teaches each of us not to look down on ourselves because of the lowly positions we may hold. Instead, we must remember that most constructive change often starts at the bottom, and God can use *anyone* who is available to speak to the Zedekiahs of the world.

Because of lowly Ebed-melech, the same king who had granted four of his influential advisers permission to place Jeremiah in the dungeon now gave Ebed-melech an order to take thirty men to pull Jeremiah up out of the deep dungeon. The dungeon was so deep that thirty strong, skilled, sensitive men—trained to follow instructions and disciplined to work together as a team—were needed to lift up God's prophet. Indeed, prophetic ministry requires strong, loyal, dependable, united, focused, and dedicated supporters.

These thirty men remind us that it always requires more help to do good than to do evil. Note also that the thirty men the king summoned remained anonymous. Apparently they did not need any photo ops with Jeremiah and Ebed-melech. They were content to know what to do, when to do it, and where to do it for the success of prophetic ministry.

In addition to the resources of thirty men, Ebed-melech was challenged to use his own creativity and imagination. He went into the king's house and found some old, discarded rags and some rope to use to pull Jeremiah out of the dungeon. This ought to remind us that some things that are thrown away—considered useless—are often things to which we have to return to complete a new task. The new may be good, but we must not forget the old that helped us to get where we are.

Our foremothers and forefathers did not have the luxury of the new. They were forced to use only what they had for God to make a way out of no way. But when people are determined to succeed, they will be creative with what they have. They will trust God with rags, with leftovers, with "throwaways" to lift others from their dungeons of muck and mire.

Imagine Ebed-melech saying, "We are here to help you, Jeremiah. Be patient, I have the king's blessings and thirty strong men, along with some rags and rope. Jeremiah, your prayers have been answered. Help has come. Your career will begin again. Your prophetic voice will ring again in Judah with the sound of a trumpet. Your enemies thought they had put you down for good. But God lifted you. God is not through with you yet. God has much more work for you to do. Jeremiah, you must speak again with prophetic power and prophetic courage. You must speak until justice wakes, rubs sleep from its eyes, and balances the scales of history. You must speak until the wrong has been made right, till the oppressed have had their day in court, and till truth can stand tall again, clothed in righteousness."

Today the prophet of Nazareth bids each of us to speak. When he spoke, they crucified him. They lifted him high. They spread him wide. And when he died with love in his heart and forgiveness for his crucifiers, they placed him in the deep dungeon of death. There he preached prophetically to the spirits in prison, according to the epistle of Peter. But the third day, Sunday morning, God raised him.

William Cowper said it best:

God moves in a mysterious way. His wonders to perform;
He plants His footsteps in the sea
and rides upon the storm. . . .
His purpose will ripen fast, unfolding every hour:
The bud may have a bitter taste, but sweet will be the flower.

Blind belief is sure to err, and scan His works in vain:
God is His own interpreter, and He will make it plain."[2]

NOTES
1. Attributed to Daniel Webster, 1823. http://en.wikiquote.org/wiki/Daniel_Webster (accessed April 5, 2006).
2. William Cowper, "God Moves in a Mysterious Way," in John Newton, *Twenty-six Letters on Religious Subjects,* 1774, http://www.cyberhymnal.org/htm/g/m/gmovesmw.htm (accessed April 5, 2006).

[5]
HOW SHOULD WE TREAT
OUR ENEMIES?[1]

Based on Matthew 5:44-46

O daughter of Babylon, you devastated one,
How blessed will be the one who repays you
With the recompense with which you have repaid us.
How blessed will be the one who seizes
   and dashes your little ones
Against the rock.
Psalm 137:8-9 NASB

I HEARD A FOX TELEVISION REPORTER CALL THE PICTURES OF death and destruction in Baghdad "spectacular." Those who were with me in Oakland's Foothill Barbershop said, "Why didn't he say 'horrifying' or 'mortifying'?" Did he really enjoy the bombing of God's children who live in Baghdad?

What does the religion of Jesus teach about how we ought to relate to our enemies? Jesus taught us the Golden Rule: "Do to others what you would have them do to you" (Matthew 7:12 NIV). In contrast, the powerful and the strong say, "Do to others as you *think* they might do to you, but make sure to do it first."

In the name of peace and in the cause of liberating the oppressed people of Iraq from a demonic leader, our nation proceeded to bomb their innocent citizens and blow up their buildings. In the name of our holy flag, we self-righteous and sinless, patriotic Americans substitute "Iraq" for "Babylon" in Psalm 137:8-9 and say:

O daughter of [Iraq], you devastated one,
How blessed will be the one who repays you
With the recompense with which you have repaid us.
How blessed will be the one who seizes
   and dashes your little ones
Against the rock.

People love to use power against an enemy. Consequently, Jesus the peacemaker is not very popular, even in many Christian circles. Many churchgoing people believe that "might makes right"; therefore, winners must fight and losers are lovers who have no might. However, winning a fight today will not necessarily prevent the losers from seeking a rematch tomorrow that will be fought on *their* terms, not ours.

Because history teaches that yesterday's losers often become tomorrow's winners, Americans should always be humble and repentant. Winners should never enjoy any personal cruelty that they heap on an enemy, because Jesus wants us to win without humiliating our enemy. Remember, whoever you humiliate has great-grandchildren, nieces, nephews, and cousins who will be waiting to heap revenge on your off-spring. Jesus taught us to refrain from enjoying our enemy's defeat and to avoid self-righteously justifying the harm that we inflict.

Those of us who quote Jesus are called un-American, unpa-triotic, disloyal to our president, and nonsupportive of our loved ones and relatives in the armed services. But we must remind people that Jesus said, "But I say unto you, Love your enemies, bless them that curse you, do good to them that hate you, and pray for them which despitefully use you, and per-secute you; that ye may be the children of your Father which is in heaven" (Matthew 5:44-45 KJV).

Nel Noddings writes in *Women and Evil*, "[P]eople, real people rarely choose evil. . . . We do evil in the name of some overriding good, usually, paradoxically the conquest of evil."[2] When we do evil in the name of good, we are doing two unjust things:

1. We are promoting our own self-interest or advancing our own agendas, or trying to look good or feel good at the expense of humiliating someone else.

2. We are demonizing the other person while denying our own imperfections, forgetting that only God is truly, authen-tically, and genuinely good.

Often, we are blind to the fact that any goodness we have is *flawed goodness.* Any goodness we model is merely a gift to us from God, and were it not for the gift of God's goodness, all of us would be less human and more animalistic in our behavior. This is suggested by the Latin phrase *Homo homini lupus*, which means, "Humankind is a wolf to humankind."

Jesus warned of false prophets who would come to us in sheep's clothing but who would inwardly be wolves. As children, we read the story of "Little Red Riding Hood" and the big, bad wolf that could speak, deceive, and destroy. In Jack London's *Call of the Wild*, when a San Francisco dog named Buck is taken to the wilds of cold Alaska, the sleeping viciousness of the wolf awakens in him. When Buck learns in that icy cold environment that, though he was reared as a dog in San Francisco, he is in reality a wolf, he becomes the head of a wolf pack that enjoys hunting animals to kill them and taste their warm blood.

Similarly, persons who were born to live in warm, loving surroundings as lambs can, in a cold and mean-spirited environment, end up as bloodthirsty wolves. Only the love of Christ beating in human hearts can convert us from enjoying cruelty to loving compassion. When the forgiving presence of Jesus Christ presides over our lives, we say farewell to hate, farewell to hostility, farewell to hellishness. When the loving power of the Holy Spirit conducts our minds as a master conducts a symphony, the melody of our lives will sing, "Welcome to forgiveness, welcome to fellowship, welcome to family."

Many families from different countries and of various colors, creeds, and classes constitute God's human family. May we remember those families in which Job's children languish in undeserved suffering. May we hear the cries of those who are criminally underfunded at the bank of justice in the world's most affluent nation. May we remember that we are prisoners chained in the cell block of media censorship by the jailers of democracy.

Lest we waste the lives of youthful soldiers whose patriotic and pure self-sacrifices prosper the rich with cost-plus contracts to sell death machines to the Pentagon and the military-industrial complex, and lest we forget about God who loved the world enough to send us Jesus, the Prince of Peace, let those of us who want fractured families healed, who want to reconcile our enemies and not enjoy their suffering, seek and meet and greet the Christ who cleans up corruption, who cures warring madness, and who creates us and re-creates us in his own image—Christ, sent from the heart of God; Christ, source of our peace; Christ, savior of our souls.

NOTES

1. This sermon was preached at Allen Temple Baptist Church on March 23, 2003, immediately after the United States declared war on Iraq.
2. Nel Noddings, *Women and Evil* (Berkeley: University of California Press, 1989), [Q1].

[6]
STAY WITH US

Based on Luke 24:28-31

As they approached the village to which they were going, Jesus acted as if he were going farther. But they urged him strongly, "Stay with us, for it is nearly evening; the day is almost over." So he went in to stay with them. When he was at the table with them, he took bread, gave thanks, broke it and began to give it to them. Then their eyes were opened and they recognized him, and he disappeared from their sight. *Luke 24:28-31 NIV*

PEOPLE WITH SOME OF THE MOST BRILLIANT MINDS IN THE world—scientists, diplomats, artists, writers, leaders in business, education, and academia—harbor souls starved for God and hearts heavy, burdened with unbelief.

The same can be said of two men traveling from Jerusalem by foot—some seven miles—to a nondescript village called Emmaus. As they walked with the rhythm of discouragement, and as they talked in the sad tones of despair, a stranger came and walked by their side. He looked at their downcast faces and posed a straightforward question: "What are you discussing together as you walk along the road?"

Cleopas answered with a question: "Are you the only visitor to Jerusalem who doesn't know what happened there? Our hopes were dashed. Our happiness was destroyed. Our helper, who called himself the Way, the Truth, and the Life, was crushed and crucified on a Roman cross alongside two criminals. Our healer of broken hearts, our herald of God's forgiving love for our sin-filled lives, our hunter of hungry and thirsty souls—who fed us fish and loaves for our bodies and the bread of life for our souls—is no longer with us. We are in 'a godless, and finally, uncontrolled situation.' Some of our companions went to the borrowed tomb where Jesus was buried, but just as the women disciples said, his body was not there."

Their problem was not a *fact* problem; it was a *faith* problem. So the stranger who was with these two men began to address their problem. "He said to them, 'How foolish you are, and how slow of heart to believe all that the prophets have spoken! Did not the Christ have to suffer these things and then enter his glory?' And beginning with Moses and all the Prophets, he explained to them what was said in all the Scriptures concerning himself" (Luke 24:25-26 NIV).

"Concerning himself" is a revealing phrase. First, it reveals that the stranger who was with them was Christ. Christ often travels with those of us who would be prophets, unrecognized, unknown, and unnoticed. Hence, you and I are really never alone. Second, the phrase "concerning himself" reveals to us that human knowledge is limited. The stranger, the unrecognized Christ, calls human knowledge foolishness. It is foolishness because it prevents us from believing: "How foolish you are, and how slow of heart to believe all that the prophets have spoken!" Jesus, the stranger, challenges us to replace limited human knowledge with the unlimited wisdom of God. Third, the phrase "concerning himself" reveals to us the truth that Christ is the key to opening the meaning of the Scriptures. You and I must read the Scriptures through the eyes of Jesus if they are to be understood as Christian Scriptures. Read through any other eyes, the Scriptures might be considered anything but Christian.

After learning from Jesus, the two men came to their village destination. Jesus acted as if he were going farther. But they pleaded, "Stay with us. Don't leave us now; we have been blessed by your presence. Don't leave us now; you have helped us on our journey. Don't leave us now; the richness of joyous fellowship abides in your presence."

So he went in to stay with them, and when they sat down at the table to eat, their eyes were opened, and they recognized that the "stranger" was Jesus. What was it that opened their eyes? (Not their physical eyes, but their spiritual eyes.) The text says that it was *their* house and *their* table. Nevertheless, in *their* house, Jesus became the host, and they became his guests. Jesus, the host in their home, took bread and gave thanks.

But the host also became the servant. As a servant, Jesus broke bread and served it to them in their home, not only feeding their bodies and souls, but providing for them the very thing they needed, the same thing that all God-starved souls seek: the warming of their hearts. After supping with Jesus, the world of these men was no longer a cold, empty, lonely place. They joyously exclaimed, "Were not our hearts burning within us while he talked with us on the road and opened the Scriptures to us?"

For those who seek to be prophets, the road will sometimes seem long and lonely. We will need to embrace God's presence, to find and recognize Jesus at our side. We will need to pray:

Stay with us, Lord, until our eyes can see and our ears can hear. Stay with us until our souls are fed and our hearts can love; until our spirits are brave and our hands can serve. Stay with us until we can feel the warmth of your presence and the power of your Holy Spirit. Stay with us until we, too, can go back to Jerusalem and tell others, "Christ lives. We know Christ lives. We broke bread with Christ." Give us courage to proclaim your Word in a dry and thirsty land.

[7]
ON PREACHING
THE CROSS

Based on 1 Corinthians 2:1-5

I did not come proclaiming the mystery of God to you in lofty words or wisdom. For I decided to know nothing among you except Jesus Christ, and him crucified.
1 Corinthians 2:1-2

POPULAR PREACHERS ON THE AMERICAN SCENE SEEM TO BE STEERing clear of preaching the cross of the Lord Jesus Christ. It seems that in order for preachers sought after by Main Street to succeed in attracting the masses, they need to avoid preaching about the one who, according to the Scriptures, died for our sins.

After all, people are attracted to practical preaching, that is, preaching designed to address human problems with human solutions. People love to hear preachers who make them forget present pain. They want the good news of peace, joy, and contentment that is soon to be theirs. When people come with the burdens and cares of the week, they want the preacher to untie the Gordian knot of misery in favor of a God who assures them of prosperity. The god many seek today is the deity of upward social class mobility and middle-class prosperity. These listeners' hearts are not tuned to hear about the blood and gore of a Palestinian Jew dying helplessly and hopelessly on a Roman cross.

Nor do people these days want to be reminded of the continuing crucifixions of the innocent who fight in wars hatched by the sophisticated lies of modern-day pharaohs or of the peasants in the two-thirds world who die from malnutrition, polluted water, toxic waste, and the economic exploitation of political tyrants who are bone of their own bone and flesh of their flesh. Hollywood preachers, therefore, to market their messages in an age of praise songs and pop gospel music, must place entertainment in worship high above ushering their followers into the presence of the God of holy love, whose Son sacrificed his life that the world would have life more abundantly here and eternally.

If the preaching of the cross is unpopular, if prosperity gospel and peace of mind preaching are preferred, if the most sought-after preachers on the "entertainment circuit" are those who are dramatic and charismatic, and if preaching about social justice for the last, the least, and the left out offends middle-class Christians with status quo values, what must preachers do who are loyal to preaching faithfully the biblical message with textual integrity?

Peter Taylor Forsyth, the late pastor, preacher, professor, and principal of Hackney Theological College from 1901 to

1921, addresses all of these concerns in a classic called *Positive Preaching and the Modern Mind*:

> Where your object is to secure your audience, rather than your Gospel, preaching is sure to suffer. . . . It is one thing to have to rouse or persuade people to do something, to put themselves into something; it is another to have to induce them to trust somebody and renounce themselves for him. . . . The note of the preacher is the Gospel of a Savior. The orator stirs [people] to rally, the preacher invites them to be redeemed. Demosthenes fires his audience to attack Philip straightway; Paul stirs them to die and rise with Christ. The orator, at most, may urge [people] to love their brother [and sister], the preacher beseeches them first to be reconciled to their Father.[1]

Forsyth says that we must preach Christ and not preach *about* Christ. We must place Christ before people. Christ, and not our oratory, draws persons to God. We cannot coax or bully people into decision.

Christ creates faith in the will of gospel hearers. Christ anoints and empowers those who preach to gospel hearers. Christ reconciles sinners to the God of holy love. Christ redeems our past from the scourge of sin. Christ redeems our present from the power of sin. Christ redeems our future from the penalty of sin.

We live in a world where many children, youth, and young

adults have no knowledge of Jesus Christ as their Lord and Savior. They do not know Jesus Christ as the Lord of history. They do not know Jesus Christ as the one who heals the brokenhearted, as the one who preaches deliverance to the captives of hate, violence, and drugs, as the one who opens the eyes of those blinded by racism, sexism, classism, nationalism, militarism, and materialism.

These young people listen to the gospel of rap. They know from memory the lines and rhymes of the rappers. They can quote them with passion and power. These rap lyrics profane the sacred and make sacred the profane. Some rappers call themselves the "5-percenters" and see themselves as gods. We would call them little Christs. Only a few Christian rappers contend against the unholy ethics of dirty rap with the good news of the holy love of a God who redeems us from self-destruction through the death of Jesus Christ. But Christian rappers are fighting an uphill battle. Many of them are not welcome in our local churches, and some who are welcome have only a theology of conversion and not one of discipleship and Christian nurture. With the help of the church, Christian rappers need to develop rap messages that will teach young people the art of living for Christ in a world that is unlike Christ.

Who is on target with a message to a rap generation? Do the prosperity gospel and the peace of mind gospel address the theology of the rappers? Does a kingdom of God theology dialogue with disaffected young people who have a secular gospel?

What preaching is needed for a world of secular and religious diversity? In this world of 5-percenters and no-percenters, one writer said:

First dentistry was painless, then bicycles were chainless,
Carriages were horseless, and many laws enforceless.
Next cookery was fireless, telegraphy was wireless,
Cigars were nicotineless and coffee caffeineless.

Soon oranges were seedless, the putting green was weedless,
The college boy was hatless, the proper diet fatless.
New motor roads are dustless, the latest steel is rustless,
Our tennis courts are sodless, our new religion godless.[2]

There is no substitute for the witness of a church that has been crucified, buried, and risen with the living Christ. To rise with the risen Christ does not mean that Christians are little gods or little Christs. We say to new-age believers and to 5-percenters that Christ lives in us. By faith Christ is formed in us. Paul says it in his declaration, "I am crucified with Christ: nevertheless I live; yet not I, but Christ liveth in me: and the life which I now live in the flesh I live by the faith of the Son of God, who loved me and gave himself for me" (Galatians 2:20 KJV).

If the fatal act of human beings was the crucifixion of God's Son at Calvary, and if killing God's best at Calvary was a manifestation of human beings behaving in the worst way possible, the forgiving love of Jesus for us on that cross was

God at God's best. What is there for us to preach but Jesus Christ—crucified, dead, buried, and risen again for us?

To him be glory and honor, now and forever.

NOTES

1. P. T. Forsyth. *Positive Preaching and the Modern Mind* (1907, reprint Blackwood, South Australia: New Creation, 1993), 2–3.
2. Arthur Guiterman. "The March of Science," *Gaily the Troubadour* (New York: E. P. Dutton, 1936), 38.

[8]
SAVE THE BLACK CHILD

Based on Exodus 2:1-10

When the child grew up, [the child's mother] brought him to Pharaoh's daughter, and she took him as her son. She named him Moses, "because," she said, "I drew him out of the water." *Exodus 2:10*

THE BLACK CHILD IS AT RISK. THE BLACK CHILD IS BECOMING A vanishing species. And it seems the state has only one "solution" for the "salvation" of the black child: more detention centers, jails, and prisons. They who control the shaping of budgets would rather spend $30,000 a year to house a black prisoner than $15,000 a year to send a black intellectual youth to Stanford University.

While AIDS, black-on-black street crime, drive-by shootings, deteriorating neighborhoods, and decaying schools decimate the black child, social scientists continue to write about the black family in negative ways. From Daniel Patrick Moynihan's writings in the sixties to Bill Moyers' more recent portrayal, the black family has been defined by four basic adjectives: *dysfunctional*, *disintegrating*, *destructive*, and *dying*.

In novels, movies, and the majority of television shows, the black male is presented as being undereducated, oversexed, chemically addicted, morally retarded, violently oriented, abusive to women and children, and displaced in the economic world of highly skilled and technically trained workers.

Because such destructive pronouncements provide the fatal fuel that ignites hot fires of anger and personal failure in the black child, thankfully, experts such as Harriet McAdoo Pipes, Robert Staples, and Andrew Billingsley present a more balanced picture of the black family by telling us about its virtues:

- dynamic with dedicated extended family and church members
- devoted to each family member
- determined to sacrifice and share
- divinely motivated with a moral and spiritual agenda

Scholars such as Jacquelyn Grant, J. Deotis Roberts, and C. Eric Lincoln have reminded us that the church has been an extended family within the black community and that it must do more than it has ever done to save the black child. Today more than ever, we need black pastors and churches to work cooperatively across denominational lines. The "One Church, One Child" program founded by Father George Clements provides such an opportunity. The Congress of National Black Churches (CNBC) offers a family-based approach in a program called Project Spirit sponsored by the

African Methodist Episcopal Church, African Methodist Episcopal Zion Church, Church of God in Christ, National Baptist Church, Incorporated, and National Baptist Church of America.

What can be done to save the black child? A study of family and extended family relationships recorded in Exodus 2:1-10 sheds some light on this deep and dark question. Moses came from the tribe of Levi. His father's name was Amram, and his mother's name was Jochebed. He had a sister named Miriam and a brother named Aaron. Around the time of Moses' birth, a wicked pharaoh did not remember the outstanding deeds of years gone by, including the deeds of Joseph, the Jewish patriarch who governed Egypt, and he feared the growing numbers of Hebrews. So the pharaoh ordered Jewish midwives to murder all the Jewish baby boys at birth.

In defiance of this cruel order, Amram and Jochebed hid Moses to preserve his life. The state wanted to practice a form of genocide known as infanticide—the killing of innocent babies. Amram and Jochebed could not turn to the state for protection because the state was the enemy they were fighting. So Jochebed constructed a security basket for Moses, hoping to float him down the Nile River to safety.

Seeing their effort to save their baby boy, God provided help for Amram and Jochebed. Two midwives, Shiprah and Puah, who feared God more than they feared the state, refused to kill Moses at birth. *God provided help*. Moses' older sister, Miriam, volunteered to watch over Moses as he floated in his little basket down the treacherous waters of the Nile River. *God provided help.* Before Moses reached land, the daughter of the enemy—Pharaoh's daughter—spied the infant in the basket. Taking pity on him, she took him under her wing and cared for him as if he were her own child. *God provided help.*

Amram and Jochebed had to place their child in God's hands, and they were not disappointed in God's response. God provided a reputable adoptive family for little Moses, whose adoptive mother, the pharaoh's daughter, was a woman of means, culture, status, and power. She possessed an unconditional love for God. She displayed high principles and deep courage in adopting Moses. This African Egyptian woman provided a good home for Moses. She even allowed him to know who he was and taught him to love his people more than he loved Egypt.

Moses' story should make us all want to do the right thing and become agents of God's provision like Shiprah and Puah and like Miriam and the pharaoh's daughter, by adopting a black child. Do the right thing: Count your many blessings and share them. Do the right thing: show your love by adopting a black child.

[9]
A CALL TO HEAL THE CLASS DIVIDE AND WIN BACK THE WORLD'S TRUST

Based on Acts 4:13

Now when they saw the boldness of Peter and John and realized that they were uneducated and ordinary men, they were amazed and recognized them as companions of Jesus.
Acts 4:13

I AM CONVINCED THAT GOD MUST BE SICK OF THE CLASS DIVISION in the African American church. I suspect that if Peter and John were in ministry today, they would be excluded from the college, seminary, convention, and conference lecture circuit because they were unlearned and ignorant men. The fact that they had been with Jesus would not count for much in present-day elitist circles where pedigree, status, and title mean everything. The split between those with authentic academic degrees and those whose inferior feelings have influenced them to purchase their degrees from diploma mills weakens the harmony, unity, and power of the African American witness and ministry in the larger society.

Some of the largest and fastest-growing churches in America are churches that have been planted and are led by persons who have not been blessed by the advantages of a college and seminary education. This highlights the tragic loss the church suffers because of the split between those with and those without degrees. Those without degrees need the information of those who have degrees. And those who have degrees need to acknowledge the Holy Spirit's charismatic gifting and anointing of those without degrees. Both have what the church needs for its own good and for the advancement of the gospel in an unbelieving world.

Yet a sharp division separates African American clergy over the issue of theological education. The majority of black clergy are informally trained for Christian ministry. Having been mentored in pastoral ministries in a church setting, or having acquired ministry skills through trial and error, the majority of successful, informally trained ministers see no need for seminary education. Instead, they seek educational enrichment at national conferences, seminars, and institutes. Others who may desire formal training cannot afford seminary education, or even if they can, they do not have the four-year college degree that fully accredited seminaries require for admission.

To complicate matters, the majority of African American churches seeking pastors will call persons without formal training if their charisma, personal charm, and oratorical skills, as well as their native leadership skills, are more attractive and magnetic than those of persons who have successfully completed a rigid course of theological and pastoral studies in a fully accredited seminary.

Unfortunately, among the clergy, some college- and seminary-trained persons have become elitist and arrogant because of their privileged education. They intentionally alienate themselves from the masses of nonformally-trained clergy. This aloofness promotes social distance and division, which give way to conflict and competition among the clergy. The beauty of the prophetic leadership of Martin Luther King Jr. was his ability to unify clergy who were different in both doctrine and class. Perhaps Dr. King was influenced by one of his greatest mentors, Benjamin Elijah Mays.

When Dr. Mays became the dean of the School of Religion at Howard University, he said:

> A caste system, whether built upon the basis of color, intellect, wealth, or ancestry, is both vicious and ungodly, and certainly has no place among those who claim to represent God on the earth. It is, therefore, the aim of the School of Religion of Howard University to produce a group of ministers who will draw no distinction between "high and low," "rich and poor," and none between "the learned" and "the unlearned," realizing that position, prestige, and power are largely accidental possessions.[1]

Dr. Mays's use of the phrase "largely accidental possessions" reminds us that we all are children of grace. We had nothing to do with whatever gifts, talents, brains, and opportunities we were born with. Thus, we should accept one another as brothers and sisters who stand on equal footing. We need one another! We can learn from one another, help one another. When we embrace others with Christ's love, the ministry of Christ will be far more effective in the world.

Furthermore, our text reminds us that people are not likely to be impressed with our schooling or our self-help skills, but they will be attracted to personalities that reflect the image of Jesus. It is Jesus Christ, not ourselves, whom we represent. Therefore, college- and seminary-trained African American clergy would do well to remember that there was a time when African Americans were not welcome in the highly recognized seminaries of white America. Yet black churches thrived, grew, and enabled their members to survive ugly, dehumanizing racism and to produce lay leaders and clergy to lead the black liberation struggle and support the many black colleges that are now members of the United Negro College Fund.

Many of the pioneer African American pastors who were denied entrance to white seminaries during the era of segregation were also too poor to attend the black schools: Howard University School of Divinity, the School of Divinity at Virginia Union University, Shaw University Divinity School, and the Interdenominational Theological Center in Atlanta. But the unaccredited schools they did attend prepared our ancestors to drink from the bitter cups while traveling the stony roads and enduring the chastening rods of legalized inequality.

These living memories from history should challenge and

charge younger non-college- and seminary-trained African American clergy and laity to make the painful sacrifice of studying in the institutions of higher learning that are available now to be the best servants of Christ they can be. It is no longer acceptable for uneducated clergy to embrace the cliché, "Open your mouth and the Holy Spirit will fill it." Just wearing the preacher suits and shoes of modern-day television megachurch preachers, memorizing their sermon tapes and CDs, and taking training shortcuts that fall short of excellence in preparation for effective ministry cannot find justification in Peter and John, who were uneducated and ordinary but who made the best of the opportunities they had. Their best opportunity, unlike ours, was access to the matchless disciple-making leadership of Jesus, who had no peers when it came to the building and molding of men and women. Our best opportunity for this will result from good, formal training.

Too many younger African American clergy reject such training. They joke that the seminary is the "cemetery," and as a result, they are often guilty of ministerial malpractice. Loving God with our minds should result in seminary-trained persons being sought out by the non-seminary-trained to serve as mentors without the non-seminary-trained feeling jealous. The seminary-trained ought to be humble and compassionate clergy who do not look down on those who enter the ministry too late in life to enroll in seminary or who do not have the academic background to meet seminary entrance requirements.

West Angeles Church of God in Christ in Los Angeles and the Allen Temple Baptist Church in Oakland both sponsor schools to equip persons with leadership skills for use in the church and society. Their educational mission, in part, is to provide an academic foundation for persons who are seeking advanced training in institutions that are fully accredited. But the mission consists also of providing thorough training to serious-minded, studious persons who, for one reason or another, are not bound for seminary. These persons learn to provide transformational ministry in a world where persons are in need of the life-changing power of the gospel of Jesus Christ. Remember that Christian higher education should never be about status profiling but about serving a needy world with the mind and mission of Jesus Christ.

Because we are saved by grace, and not by our formal education, there should be no chasm between formally- and nonformally-trained clergy. If both categories of clergy have been with Jesus, then those with degrees and those without them will realize that it is Jesus who makes a difference in their lives. It is Jesus who makes them members of one another. We cannot deny that when it comes to truly knowing Jesus, each of us, irrespective of formal training, is in some ways unlearned and ignorant. No matter how much we may know about Jesus, there remains much more to learn. The mysteries of the faith and the complexities of living in a world of perplexities should humble us to the point of desiring to unite the fragments of our individual intellectual attainments for the good of the whole body of Christ.

Martin Luther King Jr. was not an elitist. He lived a modest, simple life. He did not spend large sums of money for his clothes. He drove a Chevrolet. He challenged his college fraternity brothers and his upward mobility–focused peers to seek justice for the poor in America and in the two-thirds world. Dr. King's lifestyle should awaken our sleeping consciences.

We do not need to push and promote our differences. We must push and promote our commonality, because God uses all of our unique qualities to harmonize our gifts for the common good. Professor Ralph E. Luker illustrates the richness of black clergy diversity in his comparison of Vernon Johns and Martin Luther King Jr.:

> Vernon Johns and King differed in remarkable ways. Johns was born in the rural South and found city life distasteful; whereas, King was born in the urban South and won his greatest victories in its cities. Johns was of the generation of King's father and died in the midst of the civil rights crusade; whereas, King's generation gave the movement its leadership in large numbers and some historians date its end at his death.
>
> Johns was an enthusiastic spokesman for black capitalism; whereas, King was a critic of capitalism's economic disparities. Johns advocated armed self-defense for communities of color in the South; whereas, King hoped the South could become a peaceful kingdom through aggressive nonviolent protest.
>
> Johns' congregations sometimes drove him from their pulpit, only subsequently to rehire him; whereas, either of King's congregations would have happily made him their pastor into eternity.[2]

Both Vernon Napoleon Johns and Martin Luther King Jr. were prophets. Johns was a pastor and former president of Virginia Theological Seminary and College in Lynchburg. He paved the way for King's ministry in Montgomery, Alabama. He was a mentor of Wyatt Tee Walker and Ralph David Abernathy. King was proud to be called the successor of Johns at Dexter Avenue Baptist Church in Montgomery.[3] King was wise enough to appreciate Johns, and he drew wisdom and inspiration from Johns's sermons.

Let us strive to be as vigilant as Dr. King was in working to heal our society. Such striving requires that we heal as many areas of division in the church as we can. After all, education is not the only issue that divides us. There is also the fragmentation in the African American church that results from such factors as regionalism and economics. For example, I have seen those who attend a seminary located in a certain geographic area flock together to prevent persons who attend a school located outside their region from being called to serve as pastors in certain prestigious pulpits. Another problem is that pastors of smaller churches are not considered successful unless their churches are located in academic communities. Still another issue is that gifted clergy who serve on pastoral staffs or who are in specialized ministries (such as prison, hospital, or campus ministry chaplains) or who serve as overseas missionaries are looked down upon by African American clergy and laity because the African American Christian community regards the ministry of the senior church pastor as the one, true call to Christian ministry.

Another problem that exists among senior pastors is the division between those who are in demand as pulpit preaching stars (and who are thus on center stage as entertaining and motivational speakers) and those who are thoughtful teaching preachers, dedicated not mainly to impress but rather to inform their hearers about the call to discipleship and the meaning of Christian commitment.

Still another issue is that success in the African American pulpit is typically defined in terms of serving the middle class, upwardly mobile population. In contrast, Jesus defined success in terms of preaching the gospel to the poor, healing the brokenhearted, preaching deliverance to the captives and recovery of sight to the blind, setting at liberty those that are bruised, and preaching the acceptable year of the Lord (Luke 4:18).

A newspaper story revealed startling statistics from a study of 1,002 American adults conducted by Gallup for the California Nurses Association. The poll was taken to determine the professions that the public trusts the most. The results showed that nurses were deemed trustworthy by 82 percent of those surveyed, pharmacists by 67 percent, medical doctors by 65 percent, high school teachers by 64 percent, police officers by 61 percent, and clergy by 54 percent.[4]

The fact that clergy ranked lowest suggests that *all* clergy, irrespective of class or culture, must work harder to practice the ethics of caring and compassion if the public once again is to view the clergy as being worthy of its trust. Clergy leaders cannot promote cultural wars. Nor can they forget the loving spirit of Jesus Christ by calling for any public policy that endorses militarism, global domination, ruthless selfishness, environmental destruction, and insensitivity to the needs of the poor. Clergy must be seen as persons who work together to make life more humane and sacred instead of being seen as persons who fight among themselves. In the Spirit of Jesus Christ, clergy must flee from demeaning and denigrating people whose lifestyles differ from the norms of the masses or whose religions are rooted in non-Christian soil. Let clergy practice the deeds of Jesus of Nazareth. Let clergy endeavor to act justly, love mercy, and walk humbly with God.

In sum, Abraham Joshua Heschel, the prolific writer on the prophets, reminds us that in regard to cruelties committed in the name of a free society, some are guilty while all are responsible.[5] This being the case, clergy, as leaders, must unite through prophetic action to win back the world's trust.

NOTES
1. Randall M. Jelks, "Benjamin Elijah Mays and the Creation of an Insurgent Negro Professional Clergy," *AME Review*, July–September 2002, 35.
2. Ralph E. Luker, "Johns the Baptist: A Profile of Vernon N. Johns," *AME Review,* July–September 2002, 26.
3. "Letter from Martin Luther King Jr. to Howard Thurman (October 31, 1955)," *The Papers of Martin Luther King*, vol. 2, ed. Clayborne Carson, Ralph E. Luker, Penny A. Russell, and Peter Holloran (Berkeley: University of California Press, 1994), 583.
4. "Healthcare is key in congressional race," *Chicago Daily Herald*, February 12, 2006, 6.
5. Michael Lerner, *The Left Hand of God: Taking Back Our Country from the Religious Right* (San Francisco: HarperSanFrancisco, 2006), 324.

[10]
LET HULDAH TELL IT

Based on 2 Kings 22:1-20 and Acts 2:17-21

There is no longer Jew or Greek, there is no longer slave or free, there is no longer male and female; for all of you are one in Christ Jesus.
Galatians 3:28

DEMETRIUS K. WILLIAMS IS A NATIONAL BAPTIST WHO TEACHES AT a Roman Catholic university in New Orleans. Before we ask what he has to teach Roman Catholics at Tulane University, let us ask what he has to teach Protestants, especially Baptists, in the free church tradition. His book *An End to This Strife* has caught my eye and ear and has also captured my heart. Some clergy and laypersons of the African American church might not respond as warmly to his challenge as I have. They might reject his prescription for the prophetic tradition—one that has typically been used to critique racism and classism perpetrated historically *against* African Americans—a call to turn inward and critique the sexist practices *among* African Americans in our churches. The African American religious tradition of struggle against racism and classism is inconsistent and incomplete until it addresses sexism with the same vigor and attention.[1]

Cheryl Townsend Gilkes best explains why some persons would disagree with Demetrius K. Williams and those of us who support his views. According to Gilkes, "[S]ubordination and subservience were evident problems [in the black church] but not silence, isolation, and exclusion."[2] In other words, she acknowledges that women have been subordinated in African American churches, but she disagrees with Williams that they have been silenced, isolated, or excluded. The assertion that women have not been silenced, isolated, or excluded may lead some to believe that everything is all right with respect to their treatment, but this is not the case, because any form of subordination based on gender is evidence of inequality. Unequal treatment of women contradicts the Bible, which calls us to prophetic action in implementing gender justice (see 2 Kings 22:1-20; Acts 2:17-21; Galatians 3:28).

Those who disagree with Cheryl Townsend Gilkes may want to ask if they have examined their practices with respect to race and class. If they have no issues with race, how Christian are they in accepting persons of a lower socioeconomic class? Have we as church leaders and members failed to address prophetically the issues of gender and women in ministry because we have not made peace with God on the issues of race and class? Let us examine the prophetic challenge to these issues that comes from Galatians 3:28: "There is no longer Jew or Greek, there is no longer slave or free, there is no longer male and female; for all of you are one in Christ Jesus." Jew and Gentile race classifications, slave and free class designations, and male and female gender separations are all unified, harmonized, and made one in Christ. Acts 2:17-18 speaks with specific clarity on the issue of gender equality in the ministry of proclamation:

"In the last days, God said,
I will pour out my Spirit upon all people.
Your sons and daughters will prophesy,
your young men will see visions,
and your old men will dream dreams.
In those days I will pour out my Spirit
upon *all my servants*, men and women alike,
and they will prophesy."
NLT, emphasis added

As early as the nineteenth century, Jarena Lee, the second black woman to preach in recorded history, spoke prophetic words to Bishop Richard Allen of the African Methodist Episcopal Church: "Oh how careful we ought to be, lest through our by-laws of church government and discipline, we bring into disrepute even the word of life. Why should it be thought impossible, heterodox, or improper, for a woman to preach, seeing that the Savior died for the woman as well as the man?"[3]

How short was the memory of black male preachers who stood against Jarena Lee and the women clergy of her day, women such as Zilphaw Elaw and Julia Foote. Those short memories made those black men forget that during slavery, slave preachers were not allowed to preach unless they were supervised by white preachers. Our short memories do not excuse us from harming innocent ones, who are not responsible for their gender, with the destructive and degrading treatment we have received from others.

It would be wise on our parts if we could learn from twenty-six-year-old King Josiah, who inherited the throne of Judah at the age of eight. Josiah succeeded Amon, his father, who was a wicked king. His mother was Jedidah, and his grandfather was Manasseh, who had become king when he was twelve years old. Like his son, Amon, Manasseh was wicked. He ignored the prophets and consulted mediums and psychics. He desecrated the temple of the Lord and erected an image to Asherah, a Canaanite mother goddess who was a mistress to Baal. He sacrificed his son in the fire. Tradition says that Manasseh sawed Isaiah in two when he was trying to hide in a hollow log. Josiah's father and grandfather did not love God, but Hezekiah, Josiah's great-great-grandfather, was a God-fearing, praying leader who trusted God. He became king at the age of twenty-five, and he led Judah for twenty-nine years. Hezekiah was said to be the greatest king in trusting God; his great-great-grandson, Josiah, was said to be the greatest king in obeying the law of God.

When Josiah was twenty-six years old, he instructed the high priest Hilkiah to repair the temple. While the carpenters, masons, and builders were at work in the house of God, a lost book turned up. That book was the Book of the Law. Hilkiah gave the book to Shaphan, the secretary of the king's court, who in turn gave the book to the king. King Josiah said,

"Read to me from the book." Although there were many books, the king did not want just any book read to him. He wanted Shaphan to read to him from *the Book*.

Human creativity has resulted in books that fill libraries and bookstores. But only God's Word is *the Book*. Jean Jacques Rousseau, a French educational philosopher, said, "Peruse the books of philosophers with all their pomp of diction, how meager, how contemptible are they when compared with the scriptures. The majesty of the scriptures strikes me with administration."[4] The majesty of the Scriptures touched the moral consciousness of King Josiah. He tore his clothes in repentance and despair when he realized how corrupt his nation was. He sought the mercy and forgiveness of God and commanded five of his trusted leaders and assistants to speak to the Lord for him and the nation. These five men went to the home of the prophet Huldah, the wife of Shallum, for consultation. She interpreted the Book of the Law. She did what Hilkiah could not do, so Hilkiah and the four other trusted leaders humbled themselves to consult with Huldah, the woman prophet. Huldah gave them a word of judgment and a word of promise.

First, Huldah made known the word of judgment: disaster would strike the city because sin must be punished. Then she imparted the word of promise: God would not allow Jerusalem to be destroyed until after Josiah's death. "'I will not send the promised disaster against this city until you have died and been buried in peace. You will not see the disaster I am going to bring on this place.' So they took her message back to the king" (2 Kings 22:20 NLT).

Because a woman prophet motivated King Josiah to institute reforms, he first restored the book of God's law to a central place in the temple. (How sad it is when God's book is lost in God's house. How correct it is when God's book is the rule and guide for our worship and the practice of our faith.) Second, King Josiah and the people renewed their covenant with God to obey the teachings of God's book. Third, the king and the people destroyed the altars of the false gods and discontinued worshiping them. Fourth, Josiah led the people in the rediscovery of celebrating the Passover, which they had not celebrated since the time when the judges ruled in Israel.

If the prophetic proclamation of the woman prophet Huldah could inaugurate reform and revival in Judah, what could prophetic preaching by women accomplish in America and in the world today?

I say let Huldah speak for God today. Let her speak with holy boldness. Let her declare God's word of judgment and God's word of grace and mercy. Let her tell the world that Jesus is the fulfillment of a wonderful prophecy. Let her tell how he was born in a humble stable to a humble peasant girl in humble Bethlehem. He was raised in Nazareth, a town that was looked down on with disfavor and dishonor. He was rejected by his own people and became a homeless, itinerant preacher. He had to borrow money from a fish to pay his taxes. He rode on a borrowed donkey and held Passover in a borrowed upper room. Let Huldah stand today and tell how he was tried illegally at night by Annas, then sent by Annas at dawn to the high priest Caiaphas and the Sanhedrin. Let her tell how, in the early morning hours, the Sanhedrin led Jesus to Pilate, the Roman governor.

The Romans made Jesus march up to Calvary with the heavy beam of the cross on his shoulders. Let Huldah tell how, on the road to Calvary, a black man named Simon of Cyrene was made to carry the cross beam when Jesus grew tired from the tribulation of torture.

Let Huldah tell how the Christ was bruised, beaten, and bloodied. Let her tell how, while dying, he remembered to secure a son for his mother and didn't fail to pray for his enemies. Let Huldah tell how his disciples fled while he bled, but how fragile women with strong love remained at the cross until Jesus gave his parting words, "It is finished." Let Huldah tell how Jesus was placed in the brand-new borrowed tomb of Joseph of Arimathea.

Let Huldah tell what Peter, James, and John were not present to see. Let her tell what no male disciple witnessed. Let this sister tell that early Sunday morning—fragile physically, but strong spiritually—brave, courageous, women were the first to proclaim, "The tomb is empty. Christ is risen!"

Let those of us who came to the empty tomb after our sisters say with them, Jesus is

A—the Alpha and Omega (Revelation 1:8)
B—the Bridegroom (Matthew 9:15)
C—the Chief Cornerstone (1 Peter 2:6)
D—the Desire of Nations (Haggai 2:7)
E—Emmanuel (Matthew 1:23)

F—Faithful and True (Revelation 19:11)

G—the Governor (Matthew 2:6)

H—the High Priest (Hebrews 5:10)

I—the Intercessor (Isaiah 59:16)

J—Jesus of Nazareth (John 19:19)

K—the King of Kings (Revelation 19:16)

L—the Lamb (Revelation 5:6, 8)

M—the Morning Star (Revelation 22:16)

N—the Nazarene (Matthew 2:23)

O—the Only Begotten Son (John 3:16)

P—the Prince of Peace (Isaiah 9:6); the Prince of the Kings of the Earth (Revelation 1:5)

R—the Resurrection and the Life (John 11:25)

S—the Shepherd (1 Peter 2:25); the Good Shepherd (John 10:11); the Great Shepherd (Hebrews 13:20-21)

T—the Truth (John 14:6)

V—the Vine (John 15:1-16)

W—the Word of Life (John 1:1)

Let Huldah tell it. Amen.

NOTES

1. Demetrius K. Williams, *An End to This Strife* (Minneapolis: Fortress Press, 2004), 5.

2. Cheryl Townsend Gilkes, *If It Wasn't for the Women* (New York: Orbis, 2001), 129; quoted in Williams, An End to This Strife, 107, 204.

3. William L. Andrews, *Sisters of the Spirit* (Bloomington: Indiana University Press, 1986), 36.

4. Michael C. Bere, *Bible Doctrines for Today* (Pensacola, FL: Beka Books, 1987), 59.

[11]
STRATEGIES FOR
REARING OUR CHILDREN

Based on Matthew 2:13-15, 19-23

Jesus increased in wisdom and in years, and in divine and human favor.
Luke 2:52

CHARLES ADAMS ASKS A QUESTION THAT WE CANNOT EVADE:

> What are you going to do about the fact that 50 percent of black males from age twenty-one to sixty-five are functionally illiterate, 30 percent of blacks are unemployed, 50 percent of blacks are . . . high school dropouts; 20 percent of blacks are hooked on dope; 35 percent of blacks don't belong to anything—not the Elks, the Masons, the PTA, the NAACP, the block club, or the church? Black babies are eight times more likely to get AIDS, five times more likely to land in prison, and ten times more likely to die before they have had a chance to live.[1]

All of the problems mentioned by Dr. Adams could be solved if we could develop a strategy for countering the conspiracy to kill our boys. In 1965, on his album *Rubber Soul*, John Lennon recorded a song that best describes the plight of all lost and confused males. He sang about a "nowhere man" sitting in "nowhere land" making "nowhere plans." It sounds sadly familiar.

What can be done to give purpose to lives without purpose, to redeem lives that up to now have been wasted, to give point, purpose, and power to those who are misdirected?

The Gospels of Matthew and Luke present practical strategies for countering the conspiracy to destroy our boys. The first strategy is based on a patriarchal model of integrity. Joseph, Jesus' stepfather, was a man of integrity. He was not an abusive stepfather or an abusive husband. Jesus grew up in a home where his stepfather practiced integrity. Such was the home environment of the late Dr. Martin Luther King Jr. Daddy King, as his father was affectionately called, was a model husband and father who loved, protected, and provided for his family. Daddy King exposed young Martin to upright male leaders such as Benjamin Elijah Mays and Thomas Kilgore Jr. In his writings, Dr. King shares with his readers the moral integrity and moral convictions of his strong father.

In the above-noted text, we also see stepfather Joseph exercising parental strategy by moving his family to a better environment. Joseph moved from Bethlehem to Egypt to protect Jesus from the murderous threats of Herod. As a good father, he moved his stepson from an environment of danger to an environment of safety. Whenever possible a good parent (or older brother or sister) will move into the best environment for the safety and progress of the children. If the parent cannot afford to move, the parent should do anything possible to help the child withstand the influences of the negative environment. The parent can, for example, point out to the children that life can be positive and productive right where they live if they associate with the minority, that is, those who aim for the best and the beautiful.

If you cannot leave your environment, do not curse it, and do not taste defeat. Never feel sorry for yourself, and never apologize for what you do not have. Above all, never count yourself a failure because of your environment. Instead, say with Lucy Larcom, a black New England poet:

If the world seems cold to you,
Kindle fires to warm it!
Let their comfort hide from view
Winters that deform it.
Hearts as frozen as your own
To that radiance gather;
You will soon forget to moan,
"Ah, the cheerless weather!"[2]

As the apostle Paul tells us, "God hath chosen the foolish things of the world to confound the wise; and God hath chosen the weak things of the world to confound the things which are mighty" (1 Corinthians 1:27 KJV). God does not have to remove you from a negative environment for you to succeed. God can sometimes use you to be a bright light in a community of darkness. You can be in the desert, but you can keep the desert from drying up your ambition, your aspiration, your inspiration, and your motivation.

The final strategy is not the responsibility of the parent, but rather of the child who has reached an age of accountability. After a man has done his part as a father, and after the mother has done all she is able to do, the child, like Jesus, must produce. Luke 2:52 informs us that "Jesus increased in wisdom and in years, and in divine and human favor."

Jesus received integrity from Joseph, love from Mary, and grace from God. Jesus took Joseph's integrity, Mary's love, and God's grace and multiplied them with personal motivation, and God gave him a name that is above every name.

When my son was copastor of Allen Temple Baptist Church, he preached about Gail Devers, the third athlete in history to be chosen for five Olympic track teams. Ms. Devers would often worship with us. When sickness took hold of her and almost derailed her career, Ms. Devers said:

> I wasn't going to give up—the word "quit" has never been part of my vocabulary. With lots of hard work, determination, perseverance, and faith in God, I was able to resume training and regain my health. In 1992, less than seventeen months after the doctors had considered amputating my feet, I won my first gold medal in the

100-meter dash at the Olympics in Barcelona, Spain, and was named the "World's Fastest Woman." I knew I was back.[3]

After mama and papa have done their part, after the preacher and teacher have done their part, after your prayer partner and God have done their part, your strategy of personal motivation must go to work. Let *nothing* stop you, let *nobody* turn you around.

Say yes to God's purpose for your purpose-driven life. Say yes to God's presence guiding your purpose-driven life. Say yes to God's power pushing and propelling your purpose-driven life.

NOTES
1. Charles Adams, "Where Are the Men?" in Darryl D. Sims, ed., *Sound the Trumpet Again! More Messages to Empower African American Men* (Valley Forge, PA: Judson Press, 2003), 13.
2. Lucy Larcom, "What to Do," http://www.reformedreader.org/history/moore/chapter35.htm (accessed April 11, 2006).
3. http://www.gaildevers.com/biography.htm (accessed April 6, 2006).

[12]
SHEEP AMONG WOLVES[1]

Based on Matthew 10:16-23

"See, I am sending you out like sheep into the midst of wolves; so be wise as serpents and innocent as doves."
Matthew 10:16

AN UNQUESTIONABLE GOD CHOOSES QUESTIONABLE PEOPLE TO accomplish God's mission. We read in Matthew 10:2-4 of how Jesus chose arrogant Peter, pessimistic Thomas, competitive businessmen James and John (sons of Zebedee), leftist zealot Simon, and rightest tax collector Matthew. Paradoxically, Jesus unites diversity to overcome social, political, economic, and class barriers.

In Matthew 10:5-39, Jesus, the professor from Nazareth, gives three kinds of mission instructions. In verses 5-15, he gives *travel instructions*. In verses 16-23, he gives *trouble instructions*. And in verses 24-42, he gives *trust instructions*. In verse 16, our focus, Jesus moves from the paradoxical diversity of the disciples as mission personnel to the paradoxical animal attributes of the disciples as ministers in God's mission. (By "paradoxical," I mean that which is illogical, contradictory, contrasting in description and meaning.)

Jesus speaks of a harmless sheep that grazes, a dangerous wolf that is bloodthirsty, a treacherous snake that crawls, and a gentle dove that flutters away. In *The Message*, Eugene Peterson paraphrases the Greek text as follows: "Stay alert. This is hazardous work I'm assigning you. You're going to be like sheep running through a wolf pack, so don't call attention to yourselves. Be as cunning as a snake, as inoffensive as a dove." Peterson paraphrases verse 17, "Don't be naïve. Some people will impugn your motives, others will smear your reputation—just because you believe in me."

Professor Aaron J. Couch interprets the Greek word for inoffensive (*akeraioi*) to mean not only "guileless, pure or innocent," but also "singleness of purpose." Hence, he is saying to us, "Do not allow naysayers, critics, adversaries, or opponents to discourage you or cause you to lose your focus."

Martin Luther King Jr. would have interpreted our text to mean that you and I must have a tough mind and a tender heart, not a tender mind and a tough heart. Jesus says, "Be alert; be on your toes; listen to me; drown out other voices; pay attention to me. Do what I say. I am sending you."

Here the first person singular pronoun "I" calls attention to the ultimate authority in Christian ministry. In John's gospel, Jesus says to us, "You did not choose me but *I* chose you" (John 15:16). Jesus chooses and sends his disciples. We are called to go forth under the authority of Jesus Christ to minister to the lost sheep of America and the world. We are called to tell lost sheep and left out sheep about our Great Shepherd.

Our mission has risks because we, as sheep, live and move in the midst of wolves. Jesus cautions against becoming wolves in sheep's clothing. Wolves are bloodthirsty. Lambs are blessings. Wolves are liabilities. Lambs are assets. Wolves hurt. Lambs help. Wolves are heartaches. Lambs are joy bringers. Wolves are trials. Lambs are treasures.

Church history teaches us again and again that one moment we can be harmless sheep and the next moment we can become snarling wolves. Pascal, reminding us of our paradoxical nature, wrote, "Man is neither angel nor beast. Unfortunately, he who wants to act the angel often acts the beast."[2] We need to remember that, as sheep, we do not need to fight our battles. Instead, we must be wise and stay close to Jesus, the Great Shepherd.

Paradoxically, Jesus, who is our Shepherd, was also our Lamb. And at Calvary, a pack of wolves attacked our Lamb and bloodied his body. Our Lamb was slain for us, but God raised him, and now he is the Great Shepherd of the Sheep, whose rod and staff are sufficient. He is the Lion of the tribe of Judah and the Lamb with seven horns and seven eyes (Revelation 5:5-6).

In 2000 my wife, JoAnna, and I, along with some family members and the late Mary Morris, a dynamic Bible teacher in our church, led a delegation of nearly eighty persons on a Holy Land Bible tour. I remember leaving the Arab village in Perea, the location of Jacob's well, and heading toward Jerusalem, where we saw a small boy guarding the sheep at the bottom of a hill. At the top of the hill an old man was watching the small boy who was watching the sheep. We should all aspire to be as watchful and as full of care as that old man—wise as serpents and harmless as doves. And we can be confident that the Ancient of Days, the Alpha and Omega, the eternal I Am who calls and sends, will bless us and keep us. God's eternal, gracious face will smile upon us, and God will prepare a table for us to find safety, even in the presence of wolves.

So be faithful until the shadows of evening flee into the bosom of night and sleeping justice rubs sleep from her eyes to kiss the dawn of that day of which Isaiah spoke:

The wolf shall live with the lamb,
the leopard shall lie down with the kid,
the calf and the lion and the fatling together,
and a little child shall lead them."
Isaiah 11:6

Notes
1. Adapted from Dr. Smith's commencement address to the May 2005 graduating class at the American Baptist Seminary of the West in Berkeley, California.
2. Blaise Pascal. *Pensées*, Part V, #358, circa 1654–1662. Quoted in Alison Jones, ed., *Chambers Dictionary of Quotations* (Edinburgh: Larousse, 1996).

[13]
THE ENEMY WE CANNOT SEE[1]

Based on Ephesians 6:10-13

Take up the whole armor of God, so that you may be able to withstand on that evil day, and having done everything, to stand firm.
Ephesians 6:13

THE UNSEEN DOMINATES OUR LIVES. UNSEEN SOUND WAVES enable us to hear. Unseen light waves enable us to see. Unseen electric waves warm or freeze our environment. Unseen hydrogen—an invisible, colorless, odorless, tasteless gas—when combined with oxygen gives us water. When unseen hydrogen and oxygen are combined with carbon in the right proportions, we get sweet, white sugar. Gravity is invisible, but if not for gravity, nothing would stay glued to the surface of the earth but would instead drift around in space.

The unseen can be friendly or unfriendly. Bacteria visible only with a microscope transmit germs and infectious diseases when unwashed hands touch the clean hands of another person. Unfriendly germs make many persons ill with the common cold and contagious viruses.

Unfriendly and unseen rumors can corrupt economics, causing a stock to rise or fall. Unfriendly, unseen robbers with ski masks can harm you as they tiptoe in the darkness to steal what your hard-earned money has purchased. Unfriendly, unseen enemies who slander and muddy reputations can practice their own cowardly form of terrorism by destroying the good names of others.

Unseen ideas that promote negativity produce children called "hate," "terror," "murder," and "destruction." Unseen evil invades the minds of people to inspire jealousy, violence, and revenge.

How prepared are we when an invisible, unfriendly enemy surprises and shocks us with an unannounced and unwelcome visit? Paul reminds us in his letter to the Ephesians that enemies of the soul confront and challenge us on the battlefield of the soul. These hostile and harmful visitors from hell, visitors that cannot be seen with the naked eye, come unannounced to wrestle us down to our defeat and destruction.

As Paul points out in Ephesians 6:12, it is not flesh and blood that we struggle against. Rather, we contend against the unfriendly, invisible, spiritual forces of wickedness. Evil is far greater and far more sophisticated than the faces of any persons you may have seen, even those whose lips and lives are wicked to the core. Evil has its own highly structured organization designed to defy God, desecrate the holy, defeat truth, demean honest deeds, and destroy the souls of humankind.

What shall we do? Shall we resign ourselves to defeat? Paul points toward a formula for facing unfriendly unseen visitors:

"Finally, . . . be strong in the Lord and in the strength of his power," he writes in Ephesians 6:10. Some are strong in math. Some are strong in science. Some are strong in history. Some are strong in finance. Some are strong in friendships. Others are strong in their faith in their abilities. But Paul points us to the strength that is only in God.

When God gives us strength, might, and power, God makes us strong enough within to say no to the unethical demands of an unethical, popular majority. We become strong enough within to overcome trials and tribulations and to defeat unseen forces of evil. We become strong enough within to die with dignity. God's strength helps us to stand firm for righteousness when others take the easy way out.

Paul instructs that those who are strong in the Lord maintain their strength by dressing in the clothes of victorious living, by putting on the complete uniform of God. Protect yourself. Put on truth as your belt, letting it go around your waist to hold up your clothes of good character. Make sure that your vest protects your chest and your heart. Buy some good walking shoes. (The best ones are "gospel of peace" shoes for an angry world that is ever ready to settle differences by fighting.) Protect your head. Watch your ideas, thoughts, meditations, and reflections. Put on the hat of salvation that will remind you that only God's amazing grace can save you.

You will be under attack. You will be criticized—ostracized for taking unpopular stands—so you will need a shield to catch the blows and to deflect the darts of criticism directed toward you. The shield of faith has protected many a saint.

Ask our saintly mothers and our godly fathers. They will tell you that the shield of faith protected them from doubt, discouragement, and defeat. They will say they came this far by leaning on the Lord. Finally, in the storm and in the rain, in the struggle and in the strife, in sorrow and in suffering, never lose your God connection. Prayer enables us to keep our God connection intact.

Remember the words of the great hymn:

What a Friend we have in Jesus, all our sins and griefs to bear!
What a privilege to carry everything to God in prayer!
O what peace we often forfeit, O what needless pain we bear,
All because we do not carry everything to God in prayer!

Are we weak and heavy laden, cumbered with a load of care?
Precious Savior, still our refuge, take it to the Lord in prayer.
Do thy friends despise, forsake thee? Take it to the Lord in prayer!
In His arms He'll take and shield thee; thou wilt find a solace there.[2]

Notes
1. This sermon was preached at Allen Temple on October 14, 2001, in honor of Congresswoman Barbara Lee's lone vote in Congress to prevent President George W. Bush from exercising unlimited power in the war against terrorism.
2. Joseph M. Scriven, "What a Friend We Have in Jesus," 1855, public domain.

[14]
THE JUSTICE OF GOD AND ETERNAL LIFE[1]

Based on Deuteronomy 1:16-17

I charged your judges at that time: "Give the members of your community a fair hearing, and judge rightly between one person and another, whether citizen or resident alien. You must not be partial in judging; hear out the small and the great alike; you shall not be intimidated by anyone, for the judgment is God's. Any case that is too hard for you, bring to me, and I will hear it."
Deuteronomy 1:16-17

IN HER CLASSIC VERSE "BECAUSE I COULD NOT STOP FOR death," famed poet Emily Dickinson provides a relevant word to us:

Because I could not stop for Death,
He kindly stopped for me;
The carriage held but just ourselves
And Immortality.

We slowly drove, he knew no haste,
And I had put away
My labor, and my leisure too,
For his civility.

We passed the school where children played
At wrestling in a ring;
We passed the fields of gazing grain,
We passed the setting sun.

We paused before a house that seemed
A swelling of the ground;
The roof was scarcely visible,
The cornice but a mound.

Since then 'tis centuries; but each
Feels shorter than the day
I first surmised the horses' heads
Were toward eternity.[2]

   Dickinson reminds us of the fragility of life. Since life is fragile, we need to treat our lives with care. Our relationships with those who mean much to us must be protected and preserved as tender treasures.

   Death is inevitable. But when it will come for you or for me is something we do not know. And why death comes sooner for many who are in the prime of their lives and later for many whose lives seem to be occupying wasted space on earth is among the unanswered questions of our existence. This unanswered question forces us to ask many questions:

- How should we live our lives? For what purposes should we choose to live, and how can we make the most of life?
- Is life an unhappy merry-go-round, where we drown our sorrows with drugs that numb our senses or alcohol that intoxicates us from the horrors of pain?
- Is Shakespeare's Macbeth correct, that life is simply "a tale told by an idiot . . . signifying nothing," so that the means of life justify the ends of life?
- Is life simply the happiness that I can accrue from power, possessions, and pleasure?
- Is life a trip down a one-way alley of trial and error that cruelly leads to a dead end called the grave?

The life of Justice Ken Norman rejected these negative views of living. He defined "justice" in terms of what is good for the society, in terms of granting to each person the equal status of intrinsic worth.

Justice calls for health and harmony within relationships, which requires the appropriate levying of power. Justice means the eradication of all those forms of inequality that enable some to harm, exploit, and dominate others. Justice considers the degree of love that can be achieved under the pressures of conflicting interests among people who pursue their own advantage at the cost of the greater social good.

Love cannot be substituted for justice in a nonsectarian society that is not committed to the Christian ethic of "love thy neighbor." Therefore, since people need rules to guide decisions that maintain community life, justice is required. Justice provides the rules—bringing order, balance, and harmony to society. Justice at its best uses power to enforce its requirements for social welfare, but power must be used carefully because power without justice constitutes institutional injustice.

Love at its best willingly sacrifices the self for the good of others, but love without justice is irrational sentimentality and meaningless emotionalism. Therefore, in a selfish and greedy world where love is often absent, justice is most necessary. Thank God for Justice Ken Norman. His life helped community to be born from the womb of chaos and the clashing notes of conflict to be harmonized into melodies of compassion.

I know that in some areas of life evil dominates, truth is buried, and waiting justice sleeps. I know that society supports the world's best universities while terrible public schools exist in their shadows. I know that our foreign policy proclaims national self-determination while supporting dictator friends who come back to harm us. I know that our country's laissez-faire capitalism produces millionaires while encouraging dreadful poverty; it proclaims peace but initiates more wars than do other countries. But I also know that the call of the future is the call of justice. Justice is the demand arising in human consciousness that obligates the future to be different. Justice is an expectant mother, pregnant with a hope that promises us that the unfulfilled possibilities of justice will run down like rivers of water.

Brother Ken Norman was a practicing Christian. During his last days he was surrounded by a loving family and loyal friends. My final conversation with him was one in which he asked me probing questions about eternal life and the world to come. I tried to explain, to make plain the Christian view of eternal life. I told Justice Norman that when God, the Judge of the earth, enters the courtroom of heaven, in God's sinless presence we will stand as justice proceeds to prosecute us for any and all of our moral failures—forgotten or remembered. Truth and Holiness will take their turns on the witness stand to testify against us.

But when our defense attorney approaches the bench to defend us, God, the Judge of all the earth, will recognize our defense attorney: Jesus, who for goodness' sake; Jesus, who for mercy's sake; Jesus, who for love's sake; Jesus, who for the sake of meeting the high penalty of justice for our sin, speaks for you, for me, and for Ken Norman. When Jesus finishes our defense, Justice will stand up in the courtroom and say, "I'm satisfied." Truth will stand up in the courtroom and say, "I'm satisfied." Holiness will stand up in the courtroom and say, "I'm satisfied." God, the righteous Judge, will acquit and say, "The case is closed."

Then . . . love will reign supreme. Mercy will outshine justice. Righteousness and peace will have kissed each other. And Ken Norman, like a sailor who has crossed stormy seas of suffering, will enjoy that eternal home where the wicked have ceased from troubling and the weary are at rest.

Notes

1. This sermon is adapted from a tribute given to Justice Ken Norman, a judge who attended the Allen Temple Baptist Church every Sunday. He was a brilliant and popular Christian gentleman who had been a college athlete and an Olympian. He asked deep theological questions, and during a long and painful illness, he spent many moments discussing the meaning and purpose of suffering. He and I prayed together on a regular basis. This is my eulogy for him.

2. Emily Dickinson, "Part Four: Time and Eternity: XXVII," *The Complete Poems of Emily Dickinson* (Boston: Little, Brown, 1924); Bartleby.com, 2000. http://www.bartleby.com/113/ (accessed April 4, 2006).

[15]
ONE CHILD AT A TIME[1]

Based on 2 Kings 4:12-36

When the child was older, he went out one day to his father among the reapers. He complained to his father, "Oh, my head, my head!" The father said to the servant, "Carry him to his mother. . . . Then she called to her husband, and said, "Send me one of the servants and one of the donkeys, so that I may quickly go to the man of God and come back again."
2 Kings 4:18-19,22

A CHILD IS A SIGN FROM HEAVEN THAT GOD HAS NOT GIVEN UP on the world. The church is God's rainbow site of hope and promise. As goes the child, so goes the future. No wonder the destructive forces of evil work visibly and invisibly to destroy the child.

From Pharaoh's genocide of Hebrew babies in Egypt to Herod's soldiers endeavoring to kill the Christ child in Judea, the weeping and wailing of the "Rachels" of this world continues to this day. In the world of hurricanes Katrina, Rita, and Wilma, the godlessness of inhumanity toward children in general and black children in particular brings to mind the words of the Negro spiritual:

Sweet little Jesus boy,
They made you be born in a manger.
Sweet little Holy Child,
Didn't know who you was. . . .

The world treat you mean, Lord;
Treat me mean, too.
But that's how things is down here,
We didn't know 'twas you.[2]

The Christian Methodist Episcopal Church's legacy of knowing the child, loving the child, protecting the child, and educating the child is alive and well today. Sparked by the inventive mind of Bishop Henry Williamson, presiding bishop of the C.M.E. Church; fueled by the collective energy of the Council of Bishops; and energized by the passion of pastors and churches, the One Church One School ministry honors the noble tradition of C.M.E. elders of yesteryear.

The Tennessee Conference of the C.M.E. Church gave birth to Lane College in 1882. In 1883 visionary bishops Holsey, Miles, Beebe, and Lane launched Paine Institute, renamed Paine College in 1903. In 1894 the Texas C.M.E. conferences led the way in opening Texas College. In 1907 two Alabama C.M.E. conferences voted to combine Booker City High School and Thomasville High School into Miles Memorial

College in Birmingham. In the 1960s Miles College became an organizing center for the civil rights demonstrations led by Martin Luther King Jr. And on this night of October 20, 2005, we meet here in Chicago to consider anew the plight of the child, the school, and the church in the world of hurricanes Katrina, Rita, and Wilma.

We are confronted tonight by challenging studies from The Ace Center for Policy Analysis of the U.S. Department of Education, The National Center for Education Statistics, and National Postsecondary Student Aid. These studies tell us that black males, irrespective of social class, fall way behind in college enrollment. We have always known that more black young men were in prisons than in college. But now we know that race is a stronger variable in the socioeconomic equation than class. Consider that the percentage of low-income black males in college increased just 4 percent between 1995 and 2004 (from 32 to 36 percent). Compare that with a 6 percent decrease in the number of middle-income black males during the same decade (from 48 to 42 percent). For upper-income black males, there was an increase of 7 percent (from 41 to 48 percent). As you may note, although *all* black males are underrepresented in college, the discrepancy between upper-income blacks and their peers in the lower-income brackets is not as significant as you might imagine. This suggests that race, not class or income, is the ruling factor in determining achievement.

Why didn't black young men in the higher economic bracket perform better academically and represent higher percentages than black males in the middle-income level? Why are college-age black males attracted more to the Nation of Islam than to African American mainstream churches? Why aren't black church leaders asking hard questions of the U.S. Department of Education?

Under the government's No Child Left Behind program, schools must track data by race and gender, yet educators are not allowed to target the resources for the schools where the greatest needs exist. So high-achieving schools in the hills of Oakland, California, are rewarded with increased funding even though they are already supported by educational enrichment resources from wealthy parents. By contrast, the underachieving poor schools in the Oakland, California, flat-lands, where Dr. Charley Hames and I serve as pastors, are penalized with inadequate resources, larger class sizes, and less experienced teachers. To make matters worse, think of the child of color dislocated by Hurricane Katrina who is forced to relocate to a new city in a culturally unfriendly environment. Think of the fear and post-traumatic stress the student will bring to a new educational experience.

Who is best prepared to bring holistic help to the child who is a slave to his or her fate, who is condemned to face the demons and terrors of a world of Katrina, Rita, and Wilma? There is a word from the Lord to help us in times like these!

An ancient word with new treasures can be found in 2 Kings 4:12-36, where the story is recorded of a godly woman made glad by the birth of a son. But her gladness turns to sadness when the boy goes to visit his father, who is working in the fields. While there, sharp pains shoot through the boy's head, and he cries to his father, "My head, my head." Think about the child who has something wrong with his head. He cannot think clearly with a pain in his head caused by hunger. Imagine the violence that results from the thoughts manufactured by a hurting head.

The busy father who hears his son's cry does not know what to do, so he says, "This is a problem for a mother," and he sends a servant to take the child to his mother. This father reminds us of fathers who are too busy to help their children. He reminds us of abusive fathers who cause their children to suffer physically, emotionally, psychologically, and spiritually. He reminds us of absentee fathers who are in prison or the military, or those who must be away for reasons they have not chosen. Of course there are also absentee fathers who choose not to be involved with their children. Such fathers can cause a child's head to hurt.

But thank God for the mother who is wise enough to take her dead son to the right place, the bed of Elisha, the living prophet. We revere powerful, prophetic leaders, but what is needed is one living prophet. She puts the dead child on the living prophet's bed, a place of intimacy where the prophet returns at the close of a long and tiring day to lie down and be refreshed and renewed.

When the child was sick, he turned to his macho daddy, but the father sent the child to the mother, who in turn did not *send* the dead child to the prophet. Instead, in effect, she *brought* the child to the prophet. Is this what is missing today? What parent is bringing the child to the prophet? What parent is waiting for God to help her and her situation?

The husband, a practical and wise money maker, has a secular mind-set. Because he does not understand why the mother wants to visit the prophet on Mount Carmel, he says that a prophet is needed only on worship days and religious holidays. He does not know that the prophet has one church, one school, and one hospital for a boy who has pain in his head. The prophet has life for the son who dies. The prophet serves the God who has a solution for every situation.

The mother departs to Mount Carmel to visit Elisha. Then Elisha sees her coming from a distance and instructs Gehazi, his staff assistant, to look at "the Shunammite woman" with specificity and depth. But, missing the point, the servant sees only a client. He sees only a statistical need without a face, without a heart, without a soul. Therefore, when he asks the woman, "Is it well with you? Is it well with your husband? Is it well with your child?" the heartbroken woman does not give a true answer. She lies and says that it is well because she sees in the servant a secular staff person who loves his job more than the people who make his job necessary. She ignores the staff person, who has only technical skills, and comes to the pastor-prophet, who looks past her ethnicity as a Shunammite and her gender as a woman to feel the great depth of her pain. The woman plays no games with Elisha but instead reveals her true self to Pastor-Prophet Elisha, whom she trusts. Elisha receives her bitterness and disappointment with unconditional love, then sends his staff assistant out to assess the situation. The assistant then returns with the sad facts of the child's death.

When Elisha arrives at the home and is confronted with the unpleasant sight of a dead child on his bed, he sees not an impossible situation, but a pregnant possibility. Before going to work on the child, Elisha prays. He knows that he has no redemptive power. He understands that he is only a conduit of God's power. He recognizes that he is only a channel through which God's power will flow. How wonderful it is to know that God is able to use us exceedingly abundantly above our imagination to raise the dead child on whom institutions have given up.

Upon being prayerfully connected, Elisha lays his warm body upon the cold body of the dead child. Several times Elisha arises to walk the floor in prayer. Then he returns to warm the body of the child. Elisha will not give up on raising this child. Finally, at God's appointed time, the child sneezes seven times and opens his eyes. Then Elisha sends for the mother, and she receives her son, alive once more.

God is still in the blessing business. The God of Elisha can use the church to bless one child, one school, and one community. Ask Ora Lee Brown how God blessed her to help twenty-three first grade students finish high school, and how she paid for nineteen of them to complete college. In 1987 she visited Brookfield Elementary School, located in a very poor community, and she made a promise to pay for the college education of twenty-three first grade students. She was making only $45,000 annually, but she invested $10,000 of her money in the Ora Lee Brown Foundation. This $10,000 became seed money, and twelve years later she had enough to put these first graders through college. She became the counselor, mother, friend, and prayer partner of all of those children. I saw her on October 18, 2005, in Oakland's Barnes & Noble bookstore, and she said to me, "Pastor Smith. I am now working on sending my second group of first graders to college."

It doesn't take great riches. It doesn't take a committee and a task force. It doesn't take an in-depth study and a special commission. It takes an Ora Lee Brown. It takes a Bishop Henry Williamson. It takes committed churches and committed people to do what needs to be done—one church, one child, one school, one community at a time. We can do it. The question is, *will* we do it?

NOTES

1. This essay is based on a message preached on October 20, 2005, at The National One Church One School Conference of the Christian Methodist Episcopal Church, held at the Hilton Inn in Chicago.

2. Robert MacGimsey, "Sweet Little Jesus Boy," published by Carl Fischer, New York, 1934.

[APPENDIX]
A CHARGE TO THE
CONGRESSIONAL BLACK CAUCUS[1]

In memory of John J. Smith, a free nineteenth-century black man who served in the Massachusetts House of Representatives, and in honor of prominent Boston black abolitionists John Coburn and Lewis and Harriet Hayden, let us lift our hearts upward in grateful praise to the God of liberation.

IN THE WORDS OF ISAIAH, THE ANCIENT PROPHET OF THE ALPHA and the Omega, I charge you sons and daughters of W. E. B. Dubois's talented tenth to recall the rock from whence you were cut and the quarry from which you were hewn. Remember the original African American congresspersons who, though they were planted in the soil of political desolation in the desert of racism, dared to bloom like roses. You, our adored and able drum majors of justice; you, our gifted and tireless earth shakers and world movers; you, who stand majestically upon the shoulders of the first African American senator and representatives of the 41st and 42nd Congress, are foremost in our fasting and uppermost in our prayers, so that in these peculiar times of testing you will mount up with wings as eagles and soar above the gravitational forces that seek to defeat you.

I charge you to walk together in Congress and not grow weary, refreshing yourselves from the legacy of founding U.S. Senator H. R. Revels of Mississippi, Congressmen Ben J. S. Turner of Alabama, Josiah T. Walls of Florida, Joseph H. Rainey of South Carolina, R. Brown Elliot of South Carolina, Robert C. DeLarge of South Carolina, and Jefferson F. Long of Georgia. They entered Congress in 1872 with their feet on the ground, their eyes on the stars, their spirits unbroken, and the embers of their inner inspiration refusing to smolder because their souls were warmed by the inward presence of the Holy Spirit.

You, who are our best; you, who speak for us even when we fail to appreciate you; you, who are often in the minority on the great issues of today, take courage. Unseen heroes and "sheroes" cheer you from the balcony of heaven. With golden mouth Barbara Jordan and brave Shirley Chisholm stands tenacious Fannie Lou Hamer, who is no longer sick and tired of being sick and tired. Go forth with the audacity of Adam Clayton Powell. Speak with the eloquence of Sojourner Truth, the holy boldness of Ida B. Wells Barnett, the matchless political astuteness of Mary McLeod Bethune, and the wisdom of Frederick Douglass. God has called you to lead for such a time as this. Go forth from this holy space to secular space as America and the world's blessing in blackness.

Let us pray.

God of our weary years, God of our silent tears, we praise you for our wonderful public servants who place public service above self-indulging hedonism and private opulence. Forgive us for our smug, status-quo nonsupport of their costly sacrificial service. Give them formidable faith to compensate for fragile failure.

Save African Americans from competitive clannishness. As we face this upcoming presidential election, take away paralyzing pessimism and grant us energizing enthusiasm. This is our prayer in the matchless, mighty, moving name of Jesus. Amen.

NOTE

1. This speech was delivered at the U.S. Congressional Black Caucus Prayer Breakfast held at New Hope Baptist Church in Boston, Massachusetts, on July 28, 2004.

SCRIPTURE VERSIONS QUOTED